Iskra Books
Red Poetry Series

LETTERS OF GRATITUDE

I AM BECAUSE WE ARE

Iskra Books
Red Poetry Series

Leon Benson

LETTERS OF GRATITUDE

I AM BECAUSE WE ARE

Published by Iskra Books 2024

All rights reserved.
The moral rights of the authors have been asserted.

Iskra Books
www.iskrabooks.org
US | UK | Ireland

Iskra Books is an independent scholarly publisher—publishing original works of revolutionary theory, history, education, and art, as well as edited collections, new translations, and critical republications of older works.

ISBN-13: 979-8-8691-9927-0

British Library Cataloguing in Publication Data
A catalogue record for this book is available from the British Library

Library of Congress Cataloguing-in-Publication Data
A catalog record for this book is available from the Library of Congress

Cover Art and Design by Ben Stahnke

Contents

Foreword: Groundings of Gratitude \ vii
Derek R. Ford

Preface \ 1
Common + Unity

Letter 1 \ 9
HalleluYah: Leon Benson's Finally Free from Indiana Prison!

Letter 2: \ 12
The Blessings of Queen Sister

Letter 3 \ 15
Godmother Shannon

Letter 4 \ 19
Legal Dream Team

Letter 5 \ 25
I See You: The Wholeness of Indy's Conviction Integrity Unit

LETTER 6 \ 29
FAMILY TIES

LETTER 7 \ 33
THE GLOBAL ANGELS NETWORK

LETTER 8 \ 38
COMMUNITY: THE GRASSROOTS ORGANIZATIONS

LETTER 9 \ 44
IRON SHARPENS IRON:
THE BROTHERS THAT HELPED ME THROUGH

LETTER 10 \ 49
OPEN LETTER TO THE SCHOEN FAMILY:
URGENT REACH FOR RECONCILIATION

LETTER 11 \ 54
POSTSCRIPT: SMELL THE FLOWERS OF THE SOUL

ABOUT THE AUTHOR \ 61

Foreword
Groundings of Gratitude

Derek R. Ford

The U.S. incarcerates a higher percentage of its population than any other country in the world. According to the latest edition of the World Population List, as of 2021 the U.S. had "more than 2 million prisoners."[1] The Russian Federation, by contrast, has just over 430,000 people imprisoned with a population less than half than that of the U.S. The number of Black and Afrikan incarcerated people in the U.S. is almost double Russia's entire prison population. None of this is to account for other 5 million people ensnared in the state's captive mechanisms—those on parole or probation, under house arrest or wearing ankle monitors. Obviously, the mass incarceration system is under-

---

1 Helen Fair and Roy Walmsley, *World Prison Population List, 13th ed.* (London: Institute for Crime & Justice Policy Research, 2021), 2.

girded by white supremacy, but as Eugene Puryear notes, overall, it "has a clear class function, funneling poor people of all backgrounds [...] those sections of the population that the capitalist class considers most 'superfluous' from the point of view of the labor market" and that, historically, are the most oppressed and therefore rebellious sectors of the population.[2]

As an educator, questions of access to schooling and access to equal schooling inevitably come up when it comes to prisons, whether it be "recidivism" or incarceration rates. The slogan "Schools, Not Jails" or "Education, Not Incarceration" are common—and correct—refrains amongst progressives. They are right: we should invest in schools instead of jails, we should live in a society that values education and in which incarceration is unimaginable. The problems come, however, when we think that schooling and mass incarceration correspond with each other in any way, as if the reason there are 7 million people directly living under the carceral state is because of a lack of education and schooling opportunities. This erases or hides the historical production of certain populations as "criminals" or "animals," whether it be Black people, gay men, Arab or Muslim populations, etc. This reinforces the myth of meritocracy:

---

2 Eugene Puryear, *Shackled & Chained: Mass Incarceration in Capitalist America* (San Francisco: Liberation Media, 2013), 4.

that if you only took advantage of the schooling choices you had, if you only studied harder, saved more money, used your time more wisely, you too could be rich. In reality, those who have the most money do the least work. If all the bosses in your city didn't show up to work for a week, no one would notice. Now, if all the janitors didn't show up to work for a day, people would surely notice. It's the same with prisons. If the real criminals in society were imprisoned, we would have one of the lowest prison population rates in the world because we have one of the highest levels of inequality in the world. Yet the real criminals, those who bomb and invade countries all across the globe, who steal people's savings and pensions, who bankrupt entire towns and regions, who deny people access to health care and housing, are the least likely to go to prison. Why is that?

To ask the question is to answer it: there is no such "thing" as crime, and the ruling-class defines what constitutes a crime. Crime is, in the most literal sense imaginable, socially-produced, or man (and woman) made. To return to schooling, so much of what being a kid entails in the U.S. used to get you sent to time out or the principal's office; now it gets you sent to jail. Throwing a pencil across the room in a fit of rage, an example of a harmless necessary act in learning how to feel and relate to one's emotions, is attempted assault. There is no "school-to-prison-pipeline" because schools in the U.S. are already like prisons. We walk single-file against one side of the wall between classes, enter and exit through ex-ray machines, are subjected to routine search and seizures, lockdowns, and even brutality by police or "school resource officers." The reason there are so many people imprisoned is because there are so many crimes, and those crimes are selectively and brutally enforced. The simple solution to mass incarceration? Eliminate laws that define crime. Because, let's face it: even if you've never been arrested or even had an encounter with a cop, you're just an unconvincted criminal and probably even felon. Have you ever thrown away a piece of mail addressed to someone else? That's a felony right there: a "federal crime."

Focusing on prisons alone narrows our focus to the physical structures that undoubtedly do tremendous violence to our people, but are not the only ones that do so. With such a limited focus, we might forget that there is no oppression without resistance and there is no need for the ruling class to resort to force if there is no counterforce capable of not only resisting but overthrowing it. Prisons function to contain the power of the people. There would be no need for a state if it weren't for the infinite intellectual and creative capacity of the 99 percent and the clear threat they posed to the completely illogical and irrational society in which we live.

The state is a relatively recent phenomenon in human history, and it serves as a mechanism to protect the oppressing class and enforce its will over society. It does so through repressive and productive means. It represses with cops and courts, prisons and militaries, but it produces through media and schools, cultural norms and routine habits. On both counts—repression and production—it isn't seamless. Humanity can't be confined or enclosed. Harnessing that which always resists into a force capable of producing a new society is the most complex, realistic, and necessary process in the world that entails innumerable processes. One key element is the teacher, and Leon Benson is one of my favorites, one of the teachers that I, as a teacher, look up to. I urge the reader to engage this book as a series of lessons from a teacher, but not just any kind of teacher. To be more precise then, instead of lessons, they are groundings.

GROUNDING WITH GRATITUDE

Benson was incarcerated for over 24 years, which is how old Walter Rodney was when he got his PhD in 1966. Born in colonial Guyana six years before it gained political independence after centuries of colonial rule, he left for Jamaica in 1960 on a scholarship to attend the University of the West Indies in

Jamaica, a country that achieved flag independence in 1962, although the British Crown still called the shots, even if Black and West Indian people carried them out. He graduated in 1963 and shortly thereafter moved to London to study at the School of Oriental and African Studies. He and his wife, Patricia, moved to the newly-independent Tanzania governed by the socialist leader Julius Nyerere, before returning to Jamaica for another academic position. While Rodney first felt the disconnect between academia and the streets as an undergraduate, it was more pronounced in 1967. As Patricia Rodney recalls, his being was traumatized by the division "between academia and the working class," which motivated his attempt "to bridge these worlds."[3] Despite gaining a wide audience from his many spontaneous lectures, this was not a practice of the academic "enlightening" the ignorant; it was, in fact, the opposite.

Rodney was influenced by the wave of socialist and anti-colonial revolutions at the time, including the Black Power movement in the U.S. In Jamaica, he translated it into the West Indies context. After teaching about Black Power in the academy, he went to talk about it with the masses or, it might be better to say, he went to the people

---

3 Patricia Rodney, "Living the Groundings—A Personal Context," in W. Rodney, *The Groundings With my Brothers*, ed. A.T. Rodney and J.J. Benjamin (New York: Verso, 2019), 80.

to teach him about Black Power. He called his pedagogy "groundings," a term he took from his brothers in the streets and in churches, in the gutters and abandoned houses. Black Power, he argues, is part of this pedagogy, the act of "sitting-together to reason, to 'ground' as the brothers say" but, he clarifies, "to 'ground together.'"[4] Groundings exposed Rodney to the immense capacity of the most oppressed Black people in Jamaica, as he says, "with the [B]lack brothers you learn humility because they are teaching you. And you get confidence, too; you get a confidence that comes from an awareness that our people are beautiful."[5] Humility and confidence are allies, not antagonists.

All working and oppressed people are capable and creative, if only we lived in a social system that nourished that fact instead of repressed it. In fact, I learned about Rodney's pedagogy from my comrade D. Musa Springer, a teacher of mine who is a decade younger than me and doesn't have some string of letters next to their name. Rodney's groundings occurred wherever Black people gathered together to talk and were part of Black Power (although he had an expansive notion of Blackness, arguing Cuba was only country in the entire hemisphere free from white power even though most

---

4 Walter Rodney, *The Groundings with my Brothers* (New York: Verso, 2019), 67.

5 Ibid., 72.

Cubans were "white").[6] The various poetic reflections and meditations, theoretical expositions and political explanations, confessions and misgivings, certainty and vulnerability that overflow throughout this short book read like a groundings session.

My suggestion to the audience, particularly those unfamiliar with Leon or his case or the intense struggle against mass incarceration in Indiana, is that you engage them like a grounding session. You will, at the very least, learn the same humility and confidence in our people that I did. I learned both in my latest grounding with it in five sentences consisting of less than 100 words. In the 10th letter, one addressed to the relatives of the man Leon was convicted of murdering and written years prior to his liberation from prison, he writes:

> That whole trial was a mockery. Because it was based on the values of white privilege against those of poor black people. The word of one white woman, no matter how contradictory, held greater value than that of seven people of color who firmly showed that i did not kill your loved one... It's bigger than black or white, like Hip Hop artist Lil Baby sings. It's about JUSTICE for Kasey and myself. But we must see the reality of the situation without being made to be enraged by our losses or manipulative people.

Read how Leon moves from the (now) indisputable fact that his decades in prison (one decade spent in torturous conditions) were due solely

---

6 Ibid., 27.

to a racist, capitalist system to the desire to build common unity with the recipients. The system he identifies and the techniques it's developed over centuries now to repress—that is to re-press, to press again, to mold—our state of mind into resignation and hatred, isn't denied or bypassed but acknowledged and transcended. It's like watching water flowing over a rock to reach the goal that we're raised not to be able to see or conceptualize: *justice for all*. When you read in the 11th letter how Kolleen Schoen-Bunch, the sister of Kasey Schoen, reached out to Leon and how that interaction unfolded, you'll learn confidence, the belief that WE can win justice for all.

As I said, Leon Benson is one of my favorite teachers, and this introduction is my letter of gratitude to him and his comrades. The letters that follow bear witness to an individual whose potential was unleashed while enduring the state's most repressive forces; they stand as a permanent witness to the system's inability to capture the imagination and the common that is the universal condition of the spirit.

Preface

Common + Unity

Leon Benson

My humanity is bound up in yours,
for we can only be human together.
—Archbishop Desmond Tutu

> *Be thankful for what you have;*
> *you'll end up having more.*
> *If you concentrate on what you don't have,*
> *you will never, ever have enough.*
> —Oprah Winfrey

After having endured 25 years of wrongful incarceration in the state of Indiana, in February of 2023, while still incarcerated in the Correctional Industrial Facility in Pendleton, i[1] had finally come into the realization that my exoneration was

---

[1] *i* is intentionally lowercase in this book to symbolize that the unhealthy individualisms of I & Me, have lesser value than the Common Unity of the collective *We*.

going to happen any day. My confidence was realistic due to all the work done for my case by prestigious attorneys and students from the San Francisco School of Law and the Marion County Convict Integrity Union. Not to mention that my case was in the process of being decided before the court.

While my legal team, family members, and advocates were all becoming restless due to all the setbacks the decision process was having, i was calm and cool. No one had experienced all the disappointments that i had over the years. i felt something different. It was *a faith, a hope,* and even *a gratitude* in the greater good. Throughout the years i would often read this passage by W.E.B. Dubois for encouragement:

> *Through all the sorrow of the Sorrow Songs*
> *there breathes a hope*
> *—a faith in the ultimate justice of things.*
> *The minor cadences of despair*
> *change often to triumph and calm confidence.*
> *Sometimes it is faith in life,*
> *sometimes a faith in death,*
> *sometimes assurance of boundless justice*
> *in some fair world beyond.*
> *But whichever it is,*
> *the meaning is always clear:*
> *that sometime, somewhere,*
> *men will judge men by their souls*
> *and not by their skins.*
> *Is such a hope justified?*
> *Do the Sorrow Songs sing true?*

Yes, such hope is justified. This passage really resonated with me due to the injustice that i had been forced to experience. These words helped me have deeper, historical empathy for the hardships my African Ancestors endured during the Transatlantic Slave Trade, Jim Crow, and Apartheid. My empathy grew beyond their pains toward how many of them were still able to demonstrate faith, hope, and gratitude in spite of their suffering. i grew to see the strength in that type of spirituality.

My *faith* grew even more when i read books about other people like Viktor Frankl, a Holocaust and concentration camp survivor during World War II, who formed a new existential therapy that sought to find purpose despite suffering; and Nelson Mandela, who not only survived 27 years of prison due to South African Apartheid, but who became the first native South African president. While Frankl gave me the philosophy that all *individuals* have the power to choose *meaning and purpose* in any situation, Mandela gave me a *collective* philosophy that recognized humanity in all people in any situation.

Mandela's philosophy was called Ubuntu (oo-boon-too), a South African phrase meaning "humanity" or "*I am because we are.*"[2] The term

---

2 Claire E. Oppenheim, "Nelson Mandela and the Power of Ubuntu," *Religions* 3, no. 2 (2012): 369.

is derived from the phrase *umuntu ngumuntu ngabantu,* which translates as, "a person is a person through other people." Due to Mandela's notoriety, the ancient African concept was adopted into philosophy in post-apartheid South Africa, a place like parts of America, that is still recovering from a long period of political, economic, and cultural turmoil. The philosophy was developed as a way to overcome these tensions plaguing the society.

Also, i learned that Ubuntu is one of the earlier models of Restorative Justice and has 8 principles of respect, compassion, love, solidarity, sharing, reciprocity, care, and reconciliation. All these principles are for repairing relationships. My *faith* in the greater good of humanity was nurtured by the Ubuntu "*i am because we are*" and the *gratitude* that i had at that point was the love and support i had already received. From the start i had not been alone, a higher power was always present. Therefore, while waiting in limbo for my case to be ruled upon i decided to compose these "Letters of Gratitude" in the Ubuntu spirit and with the notion that we typically get what we prepare for. *Why not write as if i was already free?*

Compelled by this faith and gratitude, i began to type out this collection of heartfelt expressions of appreciation and acknowledgement on a prison issued Global Tel Link (GTL) tablet. While writing my gratitude to others i began to realize that in 24 years there were so many people that pitched in to assist my plight from different places, different backgrounds, and at different times. I could have written a book on each unique encounter and accomplishment i had with each person, but instead i chose to focus more on the most recent and central players directly involved in my exoneration, while also acknowledging that others who came before them had played a significant role in my life as well.

These letters (1-9) were written in a span of two weeks, emailed through the GTL systems to be copied, pasted, and saved for after my exoneration. Each letter is a testament to the power of human connection and the unwavering *thread of support* I received throughout my wrongful imprisonment. They convey a sense of hope, resilience, and the pursuit of justice that permeated my heart and mind amid a backdrop of hopelessness in the form of brick walls, prison cells, and barb-wire fences.

While i became more determined, creative, and spiritual throughout the years, these letters acknowledge that *i could not be who i am without community*. Through these letters you will read that this community spans from inside prison and across several continents. Each individual and group mentioned had the common unity of the pursuits of justice and personal growth. These letters also reflect the need for us all to work together in community (common + unity) in order to resolve many social, political, and economical issues that plagues our *justice impacted society*, in and beyond the Criminal Justice System in the U.S.

The letters from 1 through 9 remain original as i wrote them while inside. However, two new letters were included in this book for a broader context. One is an *Open Letter to Schoen's Family* written in 2021. This highlights one of the deepest points of where my gratitude developed in regards to the victim, Kasey Schoen and his family. One day while raging about my innocence while in a dirty, dark solitary confinement cell, it strongly occurred to me that i was still living, but Kasey was not; that my family still could hear from me, but his family could never hear from him again. This gratitude of having my life while so many others were gone allowed me to empathize more with others despite my struggles. My letter to the Schoen Family came from this type of empathy and hope for true justice to be served to Kasey and myself.

The other new letter is the *Postscript: Smell the Flowers of the Soul* as an extension of my gratitude due new perspectives and developments that i could not have foreseen while still in prison. Often when we have a chance to see or think about someone or something from a different angle, it allows us a deeper understanding and perspective. This is what happened here.

For instance, from a therapeutic and mental wellness perspective, all of these letters operate as a huge opportunity to heal as individuals and collectively. Being acknowledged for the good you have done and for who you are is very powerful. I know first-hand the feelings of being forgotten while in prison, especially while i was in solitary confinement for a decade. I don't want anyone to ever feel like i did in those times. These letters are one of my attempts to remember and remind others of the good.

In my personal practice, *spiritual gratitude* is finding and recognizing the good things in your life, no matter how small. In doing so, i found that i made the most out of the least. No one can be grateful and bitter at the same time. One of my biggest hopes in releasing these letters is that people can learn from my situation and become more grateful in their personal lives. Having gratitude for the right people and things is essential for personal and collective wellness. Something our world is always in need of.

Now that i have been free for a year, i realize that my recovery from the illness of injustice is much harder and longer than i anticipated, but by expressing my gratitude to others here, i believe it has helped me tremendously. These letters remind me that although the roads traveled in life can often feel lonely, they don't have to be by merely being grateful for one of the smallest and most powerful things each living person has: *the power of choice*.

My final hope for this writing is that it inspires others to make the choice to stand up for justice, love, healing, unity, and freedom by supporting those wrongfully incarcerated, and helping to create a more just and compassionate society. *Todah* (thank you).

In Solidarity,

LEON BENSON

Letter of Gratitude 1
HALLELUYAH
Leon Benson's Finally Free from Indiana Prison!

3/13/23[1]

Yahweh lives! Blessed be the Elohim
my rock & salvation. It is Yah who
avenges me, who puts nations under me,
& who frees me from my enemies.
You exalted me above my foes
& delivered me from violent men.
Therefore, I give thanks to you,
O' Yahweh, amongst the heathen,
& I will sing praise to your name.
He is the tower of salvation for his king,
& shows mercy to his anointed, to David,
& his seeds forever.
—2 Samuel 22: 47-51

||//||[♦]||\\||[♦]||//||[♦]||\\||[♦]||//||

---

[1] This date indicates when the author posted the letter to the public via social media.

Finally, i have ascended the tombs of Indiana prisons. Do you hear me? i am here. i am back for everything and some. All praise goes to the creator, the Most High, Yahweh. Yah-Echad (God is One)! i am literally crying tears of joy as i write this love letter to the world, while listening to the song *Krazy* by Tupac.

i no longer believe in Yah, I KNOW (him/her/them) personally. The divine spirit has been with me from the beginning, i just had to walk in the wilderness of captivity for 25 years to finally realize it.

What's even more apparent is the fact that i have not been EXONERATED only because i was innocent of the 1998 murder of Kasey Schoen, but also because i have finally BECOME the man Yah wanted to BE (cf. EL BE). All of this is evident, by the fact, that despite my enduring decades of pain and hate against me, i came out from the other end of the wash (so to speak) stronger than when i was pushed in.

i am not a broken man. i don't suffer from mental illness. i am not a bitter soul. i didn't turn into anything or anyone that was not true to who i am, like that of a quitter, coward, hater, or the broken. Yet, i am full of love, energy, creativity, and vision. This was only possible through the blessings of Yah. FIRST & FOREMOST, ALL PRAISES TO

YAHWEH.

Now, i can give thanks to everyone else involved in manifesting my freedom. Please read my LETTERS OF GRATITUDE. See y'all soon. HalleluYah. Love.

Give Me Love,

LB

Letter of Gratitude 2
THE BLESSINGS OF QUEEN SISTER

Mairiam sang to them:
"Sing to Yahweh for he is exalted.
The horse & its rider
he has hurled into the sea."
—Exodus 15:20

Queen Sis a Virgo
with a hitter with a Taurus.
—EL•BENTLY•448

★★★{♥}★★★

The biggest and longest standing supporter of my innocence and freedom was my biological sister, Valerie Buford. When i was convicted in 1999 she was a single mother to my niece, La-Dashia. And like most older adults at the time, her 17-year-old self had little-to-no understanding of my wrongful conviction nor how to bring me justice.

In the first 10 yrs of my incarceration Val came to visit me more than any other family member. She brought my niece when she was around 4 yrs old and LaDashia sung me "America the Beautiful." i thought it was cute despite the irony of the conditions i was forced to live in while in prison. Nonetheless, my niece left me with a much needed smile.

By 2009 Val had become more involved with my case, even contributing financially to hire legal representation. She connected with other supporters of the innocence movement (Tamika Sanford, Kim McCellan, etc.) and began to educate herself on the many flaws in the system and how to campaign to correct them. There were a lot of trial and errors along the way, but she stayed involved and connected.

The best ability is availability. Ok. My sister is not an IVY League educated person nor has the financial resources. But she stayed available to do what she could. And in the end that is what mattered the most.

For that and much more, she is my QUEEN SIS. i feel so blessed to have a sister that cares about me so much. Out of all the supporters i encountered before my eventual exoneration, none comes close to having a family member back me. My Queen Sis to me, is like what Moses' sister Mirriam was to him in Biblical times. HalleluYAH!

Thank you, Queen Sis. You are the truth that never died. That truth is divine love. Keep such a big heart open. It's your superpower.

Much Love,
KING BRO

Letter of Gratitude 3
GODMOTHER SHANNON

*Love doesn't mean
doing extraordinary or heroic things.
It means
knowing how to do
ordinary things with tenderness.*
—Jean Vanier

The way Shannon Coleman became an intricate part of my exoneration is extraordinary. It was like she was God/Yah sent. And this is why i call her my Godmother.

After 2018 i exhausted all the legal avenues in Indiana state courts. The only move that i believed i had left was to file a Federal Habeas Corpus under "Actual Innocent" as an attempt to overcome procedural default for my failure to file timely. i feared that i would be in prison for the remainder of the 60-year sentence.

At this point i was at the crossroads of spiritual and mental exhaustion, lacking legal resources, considering going *pro se* in federal court, and figuring out the best way for a sentence modification in state court. The strategy i came up with was to file a state clemency first before a sentence modification. People who were claiming to be advocating for me thought that it was a bad idea to file a clemency due to its little-to-none success rate. It was difficult, but i decided against the push back from others and filed a state clemency petition by the October of 2020.

While putting together my clemency petition, i wrote a post that was placed on Facebook and Change.org seeking letters of support for my clemency. From that i received 21 letters, but one stood out from the rest. It was from Shannon Coleman, a Black woman from Philadelphia, who pleaded for my release because she personally knew about the flaws of the system. She helped exonerate Anthony Wright, a man who was wrongfully convicted in 1991 for the rape and murder of 77-year-old Louis Tally.

What was even more powerful about this story was that the victim in that case, Mrs. Tally, was Shannon's great aunt. She went against the grain to help Wright after discovering so many conflicts in his case. DNA evidence would finally clear Wright of the crime in 2016.

After i wrote Shannon a thank you letter for supporting my clemency, she replied asking if she could help my case in some way. i sighed, before reaching back to her. i almost decided not to because my case had none of the DNA elements that Wright's had. Reluctantly i wrote her back to see what she had to say. i'm glad i did. We brainstormed. i would never get an answer from the state to my clemency, but by December 2020 Shannon connected me with a new Conviction Integrity Unit starting in Indianapolis in 2021. By April of 2021 i filled out and sent back the CIU's case questionnaire and by July 2021 they accepted my case for investigation.

In the course of the CIU accepting to investigate my case Shannon contacted a prior acquaintance attorney and professor, Lara Bazelon, of San Francisco School of Law, and director of the Racial Justice Clinic. Lara had interviewed Shannon for her new book entitled *Rectify: The Power of Restorative Justice, After Wrongful Conviction*, and that is how they first became acquainted. By August 2021 Bazelon became my official attorney.[1]

---

[1] Lara Bazelon, *Rectify: The Power of Restorative Justice After Wrongful Conviction* (New York: Beacon Press, 2018).

Bazelon would introduce me and my case to her assistant professor, Charlie Kleever-Nelson, and a legal team of law students, a private investigator, and a retired attorney. After working with them i grew to believe that they all took the time to see me for more than my case, but as a human being. Of course, the rest is history. Chuckles.

Godmother Shannon i THANK YOU so much for your wit, intellect, practicality, and motherly intuition. You listened to and read from me critically. You never sold me dreams of what you could do, but you did the ordinary things with the deepest of love and humanity. In the end that is what counted the most.

As a result, i will continue the legacy that your late friend Jane bestowed to you. And that is to act kindly to others in need, while knowing that the smallest efforts done with the heart of sincerity can and will change the world.

Love Always,

Leon Benson

Letter of Gratitude 4
LEGAL DREAM TEAM

Love for us means
everyone is worthy
of a life of dignity & decency—just because.
Not because of where they were born,
who they know, where they live, where they were educated...
or what size of their annual income is.
The sheer humanity of each & everyone of us
warrants our steadfast commitment
to the welling being of each other.
—Dr. Cornel West

To love is not a state; it is a direction.
—Simone Weil

{♥}~★~{♥}~♦~{♥}~★~{♥}~♦~{♥}

I had to be the most blessed innocent man in prison for my case to have been rediscovered by the Legal Dream Team of the University of San

Francisco School Law and its Racial Justice Clinic. Without the assistance of their unique legal team made up of law professor-attorneys and students, a private investigator, and a retired attorney; i am absolutely sure that i would still be suffering the deepest despair of hopelessness in an Indiana prison.

After the CIU accepted my case, my God Mother contacted an attorney on my behalf who had written about her work on Anthony Wright's case in a book. After attorney Lara Bazelon reviewed my trial transcripts on pdf files, she contacted me in August of 2021. She explained the injustice she saw in my conviction, her vast experience in exonerating the innocent from prison, and requested to represent my case pro bono. OMG.

In Oct. of 2021 i had my first visit with Lara on Zoom. It was there that i was introduced to the legal team she had organized. i met assistant professor Charlie Kleever-Nelson, Eric (private investigator), Terri (retired attorney), and Wendy (law student). They were all very welcoming and well informed on the facts of my case.

i remember leaving that initial meeting with a lot of mixed feelings. On one hand i was excited to finally have a group of enthusiastic people working on my case. And on the other hand, it was hard for me to trust and believe that a bunch of white people were so genuine in helping me.

Revisualized, Rehumanized

> I am invisible, understand,
> simply because people refuse to see me.
> When they approach me
> they see only my surroundings,
> *themselves or figments of their imagination*
> *—indeed, everything & anything except me.*
> —Ralph Ellison

Before encountering attorneys Lara and Charlie i had had bad experiences with all six of the attorneys that had been involved with my case the prior decades. They all happened to be white males too. Due to their apathetic legal performance and outright sabotage, i came to believe that they were either racist or suffered some form of implicit bias.

Since the victim, Kasey Schoen was a white male it was easy to understand why these white male attorneys could only see Schoen, his family's lost, the attack on white privilege; my conviction, denied appeals, me being a Black male, a murdering drug dealer from Michigan, a prisoner, and another convict in the system falsely claiming to be innocent. Yeah, they saw everything and everybody else, except me.

The refusal to see the REAL ME was not only the denial of these white males, but as the years passed my humanity became more invisible to the system and society as a whole. Ironically, me being misidentified by a white eyewitness during trial was symbolic of the fact that i (& others like me) had long been invisible in America. While i was held in solitary confinement for 10 years, all the hate i had experienced from white people at that point, caused me to become untrusting and unfavorable to white people in the U.$.

It should be understandable of why i had mixed feelings after my initial meeting with a legal team made up of mostly whites. However, due to the fact that Lara and Charlie were not only white, but also WOMEN, MOTHERS, attorneys, professors, and GRASS ROOTS ADVOCATES AGAINST RACIAL INJUSTICE, that it made a different impression upon me. Over the months their words of respect and actions demonstrated that they SEEN ME, BELIEVED ME, & BELIEVED IN ME. They became HOSTESSES OF HOPE.

> *It's been said*
> *that a person can live 40 days without food,*
> *4 days without water,*
> *4 minutes w/o air,*
> *but only 4 seconds without hope.*
> —JOHN C. MAXWELL

My Legal Team's belief in me and my innocence were confirmed by their actions. This gave me back my hope of freedom; that had been tragically lost after i exhausted all legal avenues. Which had me existing in a prison within a prison dying spiritually. i would grow to realize that we all live in prisons, but few can still see stars.

My Team instilled hope in me by their dedication and how fast they worked on my case. By spring of 2022 they flew to Indy to put boots on the ground. The group consisted of Lara, Charlie, law students (Jordan & Roxanne), & (p.i.) Eric. They met the CIU, interviewed witnesses, and visited the crime scene.

They discovered new evidence and aspects of my case that had not been revealed. One piece of that new evidence burst open my case. While interviewing retired detective Alan Jones he confessed to his bias and withholding of an eyewitness statement who identified and was with the real killer while committing the crime. Jones gave a sworn statement that he kept this evidence from the defense—a bold Brady violation.

After Charlie compiled all of their findings in a detailed Petition, the actual court filings would be done by Indiana attorney, Fran Watson. They recruited Watson, an Indiana University law professor and director of the Indiana Innocent Project, due to her vast experience with Indy's legal system. As a result of their nationally-unified efforts, the court granted the petition. Now I AM FREE!!!

Therefore, i give my deepest GRATITUDES to my LEGAL DREAM TEAM of Eric, Terri, & USF law students: Wendy, Jordan, Roxanne, Noah, Madison, Leigh, Nate, Kirsten, Emma, Hannah, Ron, Kali, Alison, & Alison.

Also, i give special THANKS to my attorneys Lara & Charlie because you took a chance on me and embodied the HOPE that is essential to applied HEALING JUSTICE.

For A Better World,

LEON

Letter of Gratitude 5
I SEE YOU
The Wholeness of Indy's Conviction Integrity Unit

---

*The future does not belong to those
who are content with today,
apathetic toward common problems
& their fellow man alike.
Rather it will belong to those
who can blend vision, reason,
& courage in a personal commitment to the ideals
& great enterprise of American society.*
—Robert Kennedy

[]•[]•[]•{}•[]•[]•[]

One of the cornerstones that made my exoneration absolutely possible was the founding and work of Indianapolis (Marion County Prosecutor's Office) Conviction Integrity Unit (CIU) for my case. While CIUs had been established in many other major U.$. cities in the early 2000s due to so many wrongful conviction cases coming to light due to new DNA evidence and corrupt prosecutions; the Indy CIU was not found until 2021 by the Prosecutor Ryan Mears' office, and directed by Kelly Bauder and Jessica Cicchini.

Honestly, after my Godmother first told me about this new CIU in Indy i was skeptical and didn't have confidence that they would really help me. However, ¡ reluctantly filled out and sent the CIU's questionnaire on April 18, 2021, along with this statement attached: "Although I AM BLACK, a former drug dealer, a deadbeat father, & to many a worthless son of a bitch. I AM NOT A MURDERER!"

At that point i had nothing to lose, but more hope if i didn't do something. Surprisingly, in May of 2021 the CIU had accepted my case for review. This caused me to amp up my campaign events and social media voice. So much so that Kelly of the ClU wrote to me in July asking me to stop my supporters from calling their office demanding updates, and for them to refrain from mentioning CIU's ongoing investigation of my case online. Initially i felt like Kelly's demand was another attempt of the State repressing and suppressing the truth of my innocence. Smfh.

However, in August of 2021 my new attorneys gave me the same advice. I refrained from any more detailed disclosures of my case online or anywhere else.

WHOLENESS: SEE-I-YOU

> *Wholeness is like a flower with four petals.*
> *When it opens,*
> *one discovers strength,*
> *sharing, honesty and kindness.*
> *Together these four petals*
> *create balance, harmony & beauty.*
> —MARIE BATTISTE

What became apparent to me was the integrity of the CIU through the interactions between me, Kelly, and my attorneys during the course of investigations. i believe that due to the mutual respect of each other and shared ideals of what justice should be, there was an undeniable harmony between my legal team and the CIU.

This relationship was paramount to the justice i would finally receive from the same county's court that once convicted me and denied my appeals numerous times. Even more, i felt like CIU co-director, Kelly looked at me not only as a human being, but one she empathized with. Since then to me the CIU has come to mean: "See I [am like] you [Leon]."

This empathy was affirmed after i finally met her with my counsels present during a Zoom visit in May of 2022. She had a stern appearance as we stared at each other over computer screens. But when she spoke her eyes and voice tone echoed compassion. This was especially so when she shared that she had finally found my court files that were mysteriously missing since 2003.

Eventually, after concluding the CIU's investigation Kelly submitted her findings to the Court that the State no longer saw integrity in my conviction and recommended my release.

Therefore, my gratitude and respect are deep for the entire CIU staff, including their District attorney, Ryan Mears. You embody the ideal of integrity and Restorative Justice. Meaning, you restored me back to the whole of society by clearing the injustice suffered by me and my family the last 25 yrs. Although i can never recover the time lost from my life, my exoneration is a great step in the right direction. Even more, THANK YOU, Kelly, for sharing with me the spiritual wealth of justice and humanity in your heart.

Sincerely,

LEON BENSON

Letter of Gratitude 6
FAMILY TIES

---

*A friend
loves at all times
& a brother
is born for adversity.*
—Proverbs 17:17

*Today our very survival depends
on our ability to stay awake,
to adjust to new ideas,
to remain vigilant & to face the challenge of change.
The large house in which we live
demands that we transform
this worldwide wide neighborhood
into a worldwide brotherhood [& sisterhood].*
—Dr. Martin Luther King, Jr.,
Where We Go From Here

[][][][]♦[][][][]♦[][][][][][][][]

Over the years of my struggle i came to realize that there is nothing like being supported and celebrated by your own family. However, things don't always happen the way we would like. As the years passed while i was in prison many family members grew apart from me for different reasons. The excuse that i always heard most was: "Life happens fam!"

OK. SMFH. i get it though. For this reason it is easy for me to recognize those real family ties that pulled me through in one way or another.

Firstly, much love and gratitude to my King Bro, Roderick Benson. Rod it has been a long fought battle, but you have been there for me, for the most part. i seen your face at every court hearing that i can remember, even if you had to fly from across the world to be there.

Man i really appreciated that, not to mention the many other contributions you have made for my well-being and freedom. i look forward to living free while building a better world with you as a brother while finally meeting your family.

Secondly, much love and gratitude to my Queen Daughter, Koby Bluitt. You have truly been a blessing to me. Whether graduating from college or when you drove to visit me on your own once you were old enough. I understood your plight as a young, Black woman seeking to find herself, and even you being a little distant at times. However, when you showed up—you showed out! Especially all the events and campaigning you did on my behalf in 2021. Your efforts were a part of the reason I AM FREE. Thank you.[1]

Thirdly, much love, respect, and gratitude to my Queen Mother, Yvonne Buford. You have always been there for me in the capacities that you could provide. This had a positive impact on my spirit. i have always understood where you came from and what you went through due to my wrongful incarceration. There is nothing more powerful than a mother's love, understanding, and embrace. Also, i recalled how you always believed in me and as a child you told me that i could overcome any obstacle. Now, i more than believe that. i know it. Smile. Thank you Bomba.

Fourthly, much love, gratitude, and respect to my Queen Aunt, Valerie "Tiny" Cardwell. You have had a tremendous impact on my life due to all the positive reinforcement you impressed upon me as a child. This encoded confidence was invaluable to my surviving and thriving through my carceral experience.

Early on you sent me key books that helped shape my thinking. And you wrote to me a lot. One of your letters encouraged me not to succumb

---

[1] For one example of the work they did, see *The Final Straw Radio*, "IDOC Watch, Leon Benson and Abolitionist Organizing in Indiana," 30 May 2021. Available here: https://thefinalstrawradio.noblogs.org/post/2021/05/30/idoc-watch-leon-benson-and-abolitionist-organizing-in-indiana.

to hating those who inflicted injustice upon me. In another letter you shared with me the "Goat & the Well" parable. Even more, i appreciate all the petition signatures you got from your church members. So i'm smiling because a smile travels a thousand miles and frowns ain't even getting started. Lol. Thx.

Fifthly, much love and gratitude to several other family members. My Queen Sis, Ronda Benson-Dixon. Thank you for your support and prayers. My Queen Sis, Chevon Buford. Thank you for your support early on and even helping me buy a cellphone. My Queen Daughter, Keandra Bluitt. Thank you for your support early on and for putting out that music video for my song. My King Sun, Leon Bluitt. Thank you for holding me down when you got out. We are gonna build now that i'm out. Also, much love to my cousins Christina "Tina G" Gibbs for sharing your book with me it was empowering and Lance "Rich the Ruler" Gibbs for plugging me on your I-Heart Radio show. I appreciate all the love i received from the family.

Family's Loyalty, Not Blood,

LEE

Letter of Gratitude 7
THE GLOBAL ANGEL NETWORK

Angels are the sure
& heavenly guards of the soul of man
during that uncharted & indefinite period of time
which intervenes between the death of the flesh
& the new life in the spirit abodes.
—The Urantia Book

Many people
will walk in & out of your life,
but only true friends
will leave footprints in your heart.
—Eleanor Roosevelt

One of the biggest lessons i gained while struggling to overcome injustice, or any obstacle in life, is that no one can do it alone. i was alone throughout my epic battle, but The Most High has always sent unique angels to work with me from all around the world. i now see the blessings of the many different women and men i had the chance to work with on my case. Let's call this the Global Angel Network.

ACROSS THE POND SUPPORTERS

Steve Willet (UK), Leesa Marie Taylor (AUS), Joanne Royston (UK), Leigh Golombick (AUS), Susanna Quadros (GER), Siobhan Burleigh (UK), Alina Dollat (ITALY), Katja Pumm (GER), Angela Nikolic (AUS), BriGina Edwards (UK), Tamowski-Krynicka Virginia (FR), Marina Drummer (GER), Jane Spirit (IRE), Susanna Klatt (GER), Dr. John Bond (UK), Annabelle Gabriel (FR), Dunny Cipolli (SWISS), Sigrid Davies & Family (GER) & Luke Charles (UK).

~

i deeply thank each one of you for any and all efforts you put forth on behalf of my fight for freedom. All of it was needed to push me to where I AM at today: FREE! i can't explain how much i appreciate the small and large contributions you have made to me. You have left a deep impression upon my heart and soul due to all the humanity you have shown me in the past and for those of you who are still sharing such love with me today. My gratitude is endless.

i look forward to flying out to see some of you soon. i'm already in the process of getting my passport (i no longer have a crime record). So i can travel anywhere and anytime on earth i please. None of this would be possible without any of you. ♥♥

U.$. Supporters

Leda Grace (IN), Robert Lee (CA), Anglina ADream (NY), Armen Baye Syvester (IN), Amy Montgomery (IN), Dr. Geoffrey Loftus (WA), Somone Jackson (MI), Minister Ruth Cosby-Taylor (IN), Keith Anderson (WS), Karyne Golden (NY), Dana Burns (MI), Billie Fulton (KY), Alsia Lee (DC), Michael Cruz (CA), Adam Scouten (IN), Ann Wright (NH), Eva Solano (CA), Carla Andrews (IN), Rebecca McKnight (IN), Matthew Burkett (NY), Patrick McGee (PA), Takenya Stewart (LA), Austin & Justin Blievins (IN), Kennedith Marshall (NV).

Dakari Fulton (IN), Richard Anthony (IL), Pamela Eller (OR), Daniel Combs (NC), Sonya Hennet (PA), Grave Grim (OR), Nancy Bailey (TX), Janissa Davies (AZ), Carolina Soza (CA),

Philana Homes (FL), Kenneth Furguson (MI), Michelle Schmude (WIS), BriGina Edwards (CA), Philip Shelton (MO), Ruthanne Amarteifo (IL), Louis Richard (Can), Bonnie Newman (FL), Michelle Fite (CA), Dr. Jordan Venson (DC), Angela Perry (MI), Devin Westmoorland (IN), Kayla Lawson (IN) Maggie Weigley (NY), Amani Sawari (MI), Rober Cooper (NC).

Nick Greven (IN), Sarah Fritz (IN), John Carter (IN), Nadia Fischer (OH), Ben Harris (IL), Dr. Jacquelyn Frank (IL), Devin Waldman (NY), Jermaine Conway Jr. (NV), Carol Knight (IN), Aimee Nieman (NY), Justis Malker (NC), Felix Kauffman (MA), Marissa Cote (MA), Mickey Hoover (NY), Griffin Woodard (PA), Kimberly McClellan (GA), Betsy Isaacson (NY), Sally Horrwitz (NY), Holly Rodriguez (OR).

LaDashia Frye (VA), Rafael Vaquez (CA) Lory Hannah (Can), LaShanti Overton (CA), Leonna A. Brandae (ME), Lisa Padol (NY), Eero Ruuttila (ME), James (MI), Eric Klein (NY), Robert Boyd (AZ), Cassandra Bluitt (IN), Ingri Cassel (ID), Walter Karim Goudy (CA), Kimberly Carter (VA), JayRené Teague (DE), Twanda VanDroff (SC), Jame Gallagher (NY), Fury Young (NY), Kara Morefield (VA).

~

My deepest GRATITUDES to you all. Each one of you, one time or another, bigger or smaller effort, helped contribute to my FREEDOM. You are angels to me in many ways. i look forward to meeting you soon.

Love Always,

LEON

Letter of Gratitude 8
COMMUNITY
The Grassroots Organizations

---

*A small body of determined spirits
fired up by unquenchable faith
in their mission
can alter the course of history.*
—Mahatma Gandhi

*The whole idea of compassion
is based on keen awareness
of the interdependence of all these living beings,
which are all part of one another
& all involved in one another.*
—Thomas Merton

Surely without the help and empowerment of many grassroot organizations and activists, my

FREEDOM today would not have been possible. These grassroot organizations and activists always made it clear of their common-unity with me, which equated into community (common + unity). Having a sense of community empowered me and gave me purpose, even beyond my personal needs, and to that of others.

In addition, by allowing me to be a part of the solution, in many ways i was able to contribute from a prison cell. These organizations gave me value and citizenship in a community that not only wanted me but needed me. This helped me overcome the "learned helplessness" that the system was always trying to bombard upon my mind daily. Even more, this community participation gave me a deep sense of civic duty while inside and now evermore that i have been exonerated.

Through the course of decades of imprisonment i mostly worked with the following organizations and activists:

I.D.O.C. WATCH (IN) is a prison abolitionist collective community dedicated to prisoner solidarity with society while challenging inhuman prison policy and conditions including those in solitary confinement. IW was a huge resource in helping me grow as a person and campaigning for my exoneration. Whether through organizing events and rallies, keeping me in communication by phone, appearing at my court hearings, networking, educating, letter campaigning, and allowing me to contribute to help others.

Midwest Pages % Boxcar Books (IN) offers free books by request to prisoners in Indiana and nationwide. This resource was vital to my personal education while inside. In 2018, i was allowed to create a "Changing Lives Through Literature" program while inside, but i lacked enough books for my students. i sent a request to BoxCar Books outlining the reasons why i needed the large volume of books. They promptly ordered a bulk of these books from Amazon and sent them within a week. The class went on to be successful, but not without such a contribution.

Kite Line Radio (Broadcast Opposition) (IN) is a grassroot radio show dedicated to exposing corruption in Indiana communities, prisons, governments, etc. They aired a series of my recordings of my case story in 2017. Later they allowed my daughter, Koby on their show to advocate my innocence and for the rights of female prisoners.

Walkintheseshoes.com (VA) is a website created by Kimberly Cater, not only to allow prisoner writers a voice, but to help society empathize with all people within the carceral experience and beyond. She edits the writings and helps writers become better through her thorough critiques of their work before publishing. i was given several opportunities over the years to post my writings on this site and it was fruitful.

SAN FRANCISCO BAYVIEW (NATIONAL BLACK NEWSPAPER) (SF) is a grass roots Black newspaper established by Willie & Mary Ratcliff in 1976. They cover major issues that affect the Black, Brown, and indigenous communities, as well as prisoner rights. This was the first newspaper i read that gave prisoners, not only a voice, but a networking platform as well. In 2004 SFBV was the first publication to publish my poems and writings in their Behind Enemy Lines section. i would go on to develop a strong community through SFBV.

BLACK LEAF FOODS (IN) is a vegan food service that advocates healthy lifestyle choices. They were the first Black owned vegan food service in Indianapolis, Indiana. BLF is all about community support, in 2021 they donated their catering and food service to one of my Indy events organized by my daughter, Koby and IDOC Watch.

TRUE LEAP PRESS ZINE DISTRO (CA) is a grass roots zine distribution network that provides prisoners nationwide with social, political, cultural, and gender conscious materials. This service is free of charge to prisoners. It's very empowering to read about the struggles and perspectives of other prisoners from different states and countries, whether from the past or present. In time i was able to contribute to the collective knowledge of prison struggle and abolition.

Prison Riot Radio (DEL) is a grass roots radio show run by creator and hostess, JayRené Teague, dedicated to giving prisoners a voice. Whether by allowing them to appear by phone live on the show, or a pre-recorded podcast, poems, raps, or statements to be posted on their site. i was blessed to work with PRR several times.

The Streets Don't Love You Back Org (AZ) is a grass roots org created and run by Lucinda and Robert Boyd dedicated to community outreach, prisoner's rights, and human right's period. The TSDLYB radio show featured me and my advocates several times throughout the years. Also, i worked with them to bring their Life Intervention course to Indiana prisons where i facilitated over 500 participants to graduate.

Freer Records (NY) is the first grassroots, nonprofit record label in the U.$. dedicated to the Justice Impacted community. Founded by Fury Young, since 2014 he has entered into prisons nationwide to record and produce music by incarcerated musicians and for other released. All as a means to bring awareness to the stories of the people afflicted by the New Jim Crow (mass incarceration epidemic). FREER hosts events and workshops that bring light to these carceral issues. I am currently one of FREER artists and have worked with them since 2014.[1]

||||0||||0||||||0

Sorry if i forgot to mention other organizations (American Pen, Solitary watch, Focus Initiative, Christmas Behind Bars, Changing Lives Through Literature, Shakespeare @ Pendleton, etc.). i've worked with, but i share my deepest APPRECIATION, GRATITUDE, AND RESPECT for any and all the help you give and gave to me and others. Now that i am FREE i will assist you in your continued efforts of making the world a better place by empowering Justice Impacted citizens. THANK YOU.

For A Better World,

LB

---

[1] Check out EL BENTLY 448, "Innocent Born Guilty," Freer Records.

Letter of Gratitude 9
IRON SHARPENS IRON
The Brothers Who Helped Me Through

---

*A mind is not a mind
without a culture around it.*
—Alison Jolly

*If you tremble with indignation
every time
an injustice is committed in the world,
we are comrades.*
—Che Guevara

*The highest courage
is to dare to be yourself
in the face of adversity.
Choosing right over wrong, ethics over convenience,
& truth over popularity.
These are the choices that measures your life.
Travel the path of integrity without looking back,
for there is never a wrong time
to do the right thing.*
—Supreme Understanding

[]~[]~[]~[]~[]

I couldn't end this series of thanks and appreciation without acknowledging all the comrades and brothas i met while in prison that inspired and guided me through those hard times. Some of these men have been released, some have transitioned from this life, while others still remain in the concrete and steel maze of the Prison Industrial Complex.

Nonetheless, i believe they were each essential encounters that guided me to freedom. My battle was more than through the courts; it was a spiritual and mental battle too. When i didn't receive letters, visits, or when my appeal was denied, i had real brothas who would bring me comfort and perspectives of hope.

These are the following inside brothas that guided me through one way or another through their writings, conversation, or example:

John "Balagoon" Cole, Tommy Sparks, Sean "Big Shack" Miller, Shaka Shakur, Chrisphor "Naeem" Trotter, Raylon Young, Carlos Wallance, Aaron Smith, Aaron Staton, Devon Rush, Jarvis Peele, Kevin Payton, ObadYah Yisrayl, Bravo, Bumps, Derek Williams. Anthony "Shango" Tyler, Ramar Daniels, David Newson, Janssen Hamlett.

Tarnell Nash, Paul Veal, Lavar "Richie Rich" Thomas, Jamar Minor, Nakoshi, Keith "PG" Woodson, James Durham, Philip "Popalani" Strouds, Pierce "Ruku" McDade, Kofie Ajabu, Devin George-EL, Gary "YahKim" Waters, Josiah Spears, Pizza Man, Reese Davies, Justin Hargrove, Lil Psycho, BP.

Dayon "Kwame Shakur" Miller, James "White Mike" Colliers, Daniel "Boone" Snail, Big C, Marcus Snail, Josiah Jones, Aaron Israel Isby, Cliff Elswick, David "Bilal" Amos, Walter "Karim" Goudy, Antonio Harris, Richard "Bolo" Smith, Philip "Triple H" Lee, Kevin "Rashid" Johnson, Little James, Kevin Ralley, TZ, Elder Lokmar, Shapshire-EL, Ervin Hall-Bey.

Tony Warren-Bey, Love-EL, Negro, Demetrius "MeechthaGod" Burks, Jerrel Bonds, Andre Tillman, Charles Knuchols, Malvin "Buddy" Smithson, William "OJ" Johnson, Lindale Wen, Bone, Mathew (24), Woota, Saybert Huff, Billy Adams, Brian Pace, Quon Turner, Demetris "Cifu" White, Lil Franko, Leonard "Kalfani" McQuay, Mitchel-EL.

Willis-Bey, Man Child-Bey, Larry Huncho, Francis-Bey, Charles "Manie" Carter, Jeffrey "Pay-Day" Carter, Kwali, Michael Bruno-Bey, Flip Wooten, Straw Dawg, Jerry Craig, Dustin McCowan, Brandon Stewart, Michael "Kwame Shakur" Joyner, Malcom Graham, Paris Bush, Steven Tuck, Kingmalco Washington, Chuck Adams, Big Michael Rhone, Bobby Brown, Willie Walker, ShaRico Blakey, Ira White, Paul Maze, Terry Davis, David Robert, Brandon Stewart, Terrell Carson, Curtis Jones, Thomas Edwards, etc.

~•~•~•~•

Each one of these brothas from different cultures, faiths, and backgrounds were the elements that forged the fortitude that i now possess today. i only can pray that i had a tenth of the impact on you that you have had on me. Surely, i know that i am not done learning from many of you, as we can count the apples on the tree, but not the many trees that are in an apple.

When i reflect i see this truth from all wisdom bestowed to me while a decade in solitary, sitting at the ankles of the elders like LJ, Balagoon, Naeem, Lokmar, and Bilal. It was years after i had left from around them, before some of that wisdom would take root.

As the comrade ObadYah reminded me one day: I AM, BECAUSE WE ARE. Meaning we're all standing on the shoulders of others who helped us through life one way or another. Therefore, THANK

YOU, MY BROTHAS. i only regret that i can't many of you with me, but i will never abandon the struggle while in society. HalleluYah! MUCH LOVE & RESPECT.

UHURU SASA,

LB

Letter of Gratitude 10
OPEN LETTER TO THE SCHOEN FAMILY
Urgent Reach for Reconciliation

1.11.21

> ♪*Do I have to rule the world, or will it come to me?*
> *Do I have to live in doubt, or will it turn to me?*
> *Do I have to lose my mind, 'cause it has been wandering?*
> *Will they ever let me out, I've been wondering?*
> *Help me to see/ Who can I be*
> *Help me to know/ Where I can go*
> *[Take me!] Take me out of myself again*
> *[Help me!] Help me lose control*
> *[Show me!] Show me love, show me happiness*
> *[Love me!] I can't do this on my own*♪
> —Michael Kiwanuka, "Rule the World" (1:42—2:12)

Dear Schoen Family:

I pray that my most sincere and earnest thoughts find you all in superb health and divine spirits despite the hardships that our nation has experienced in 2020 due to the COVID-19 pandemic; but even more, despite the terrible and unjustified loss of your beloved son, brother, uncle, and cousin Kasey Schoen in 1998.

You may remember me? My name is Leon Benson, the man accused and convicted of Kasey's murder. Yet, to this very day i stand before God, you, and the entire world still proclaiming my absolute innocence of that crime over 22 years later.

My intentions here are not to disrespect, upset, or patronize you in any way. Because i deeply empathize with your loss and even your sense of closure that the Indianapolis Police deceitfully gave you in my conviction. However, i love and respect you enough to challenge you to at least bring rest to Kasey's spirit—rest—if not to see an innocent man set free after he was forced to experience what death feels like on this side of life.

Now i beg you to empathize with me. By now you have seen how flawed our justice system can be. Every other week it seems like an innocent person is released from prison for crimes they did not commit. Usually it is new DNA, eyewitness, or forensic evidence that exonerates them. Sometimes they're imprisoned for decades before justice is served to them and their families. Can you imagine having such an experience?

Social Perspective

Like you, all citizens are supposed to trust our public servants of politicians, police, prosecutors, and judges. But our trust in these officials cannot be blind, due to all the corruption and scandal that has been exposed in our Information Age. Racism, greed, or indifference has been the motivating forces behind this misconduct at the expense of public integrity.

This misconduct occurred in my case. First, a Black suspect was accused of Kasey's (a white victim) death. Even today, we all know how much white life is valued over those of color. In 1998 this rare cross-racial crime brought out rage in Indianapolis, a predominately white city. Second, the alleged eyewitness (Schmitt) of the crime was a white woman. Who claimed to see a dark complexioned, Black male from 47 yards away at night shoot in Kasey's truck and run from the scene. Third, because i was Black, a drug dealer in the area, and from a different state it made me vulnerable to false accusations. Especially when Schmitt picked my photo from a lineup as a killer, even though my physical appearance (light complexion) greatly conflicted with her initial description.

The reason I AM bringing up these racial factors is to demonstrate how easily misconduct occurred against me (& Kasey) whether by malicious or implicit means. i was not convicted by the facts, but rather i was made a scapegoat of retribution for the death of a white man.

That whole trial was a mockery. Because it was based on the values of white privilege against those of poor black people. The word of one white woman, no matter how contradictory, held greater value than that of seven people of color who firmly showed that i did not kill your loved one..

It's bigger than black or white, like Hip Hop artist Lil Baby sings. It's about JUSTICE for Kasey and myself. But we must see the reality of the situation without being made to be enraged by our losses or manipulative people.

You Are Different

In no way am i accusing your family of racism. You've been made victims by a reckless urban youth and an irresponsible justice system. i have an omni-remorse for your hurt, pain, and loss. But what is so amazing, since the beginning you have had doubts about my conviction.

As early as 2003 Kasey's brother, Kyle reached out to me regarding my claims of innocence. In 2006 your family members left concerning comments on a MySpace ad page dedicated to my case. In 2017 Kasey's beloved Mother and cousin were in communication with my family. There was a lot of healing from that exchange. And in 2019 more of your relatives reached out to me directly and we developed a great respect and understanding with each other.

This shows me that you're different from most victim's family members. Not only do you have a conscience and compassion for me, but the courage to know and seek the truth. And i greatly appreciate this.

Unfortunately, nothing major has come from our communications. However, i have not been provided a proper platform, until now.

Healing Justice,

Leon Benson

Letter of Gratitude 11
POSTSCRIPT
Smell the Flowers of the Soul

---

*I've learned
that people will forget what you said,
people will forget what you did,
but people will never forget
how you made them feel.*
—Maya Angelou

*Only in a free society could right triumph in difficult times,
and could civilization record
its magnificent advancement.
In recognizing the humanity in of our fellow beings,
we pay ourselves the highest tribute.*
—Thurgood Marshall

*"In some way,
suffering ceases
to be suffering
at the moment
it finds meaning,
such as the meaning
of a sacrifice.*
—Victor Frankl

☐☐☐☐☐☐☐☐|||{•}||☐☐☐☐☐☐☐☐

I couldn't conclude these letters of gratitude without including this *PostScript*. There are several individuals and events that i feel a great amount of gratitude towards, but for very different reasons.

FIRSTLY, i want to express my deepest gratitude to the late George Floyd, who unexpectedly became a catalyst and sacrifice that played a significant role in my exoneration. His tragic murder, captured on video and shared globally through social media, served as a haunting reminder that we live in a *Justice Impacted Society*. It highlighted the urgent need for change, to ensure that innocent lives are no longer lost at the hands of police brutality or wrongful convictions. One positive outcome of Floyd's sacrifice was the establishment of new conviction integrity units (CIU) across America, which directly impacted me when the Marion County District Attorney, Ryan Mears, established the first CIU in Indiana in 2021. i humbly extend my gratitude to George Floyd and his surviving family members, because without his untimely death and the subsequent civil unrest in 2020, i would not have achieved the justice and freedom i have today. Rest in power, Brother.

SECONDLY, i must acknowledge the first official from Indianapolis, who was not part of the

CIU, to publicly apologize to me. This person is Indianapolis Mayor, Joe Hogsett, and his assistant, Hampton Shields. Less than 24 hours after my release from prison, i had a chance encounter with Shields while at P-30s (an office space hub), whom I recognized from my time in prison when he attended an inside-out program at Pendleton Correctional Facility, where he and his Indiana-Purdue University, Criminal Justice, classmates came inside to learn public speaking from my *Rising the Bars* Toastmasters Club. He was now the assistant to the Indianapolis mayor. This unexpected meeting with Shields led to a brief conversation with Mayor Hogsett, during which he apologized for my wrongful incarceration and encouraged me to share my story to help others.[1] As the months passed, i grew to respect and appreciate what Shields and Mayor Hogsett had done even more. In that moment, the mayor of the city that had once wrongfully convicted me was now welcoming me back home. This made me feel like i truly belonged in the community once again. For this, i extend my sincere thanks and respect.

THIRDLY, i was completely taken aback by

---

[1] This interaction between the author and the mayor was caught on film by Britni West. Thank you so much, Brit, for having that video camera on at all the right time. Learn more about the "Truth Never Dies" documentary at: https://filmfreeway.com/TRUTHNEVERDIES

the empathy and understanding shown to me by Kolleen Schoen-Bunch, the sister of Kasey Schoen, whose murder remained unresolved for two decades due to my wrongful conviction. We had engaged in heated exchanges on social media regarding my exoneration, which was understandable given the pain her family had endured. However, in my *Open Letter to the Schoen Family*, i expressed my deep empathy for their loss, recognizing that while i had a chance to be reunited with my loved ones, they had lost Kasey forever. Three months after my exoneration, i received word from my attorneys that Kolleen wanted to reach out to me. i didn't know what to expect. We eventually connected through Jennifer Thompson of the HEALING JUSTICE foundation and had a transformative meeting over Zoom. We cried together, laughed together, and ultimately reconciled. Kolleen had taken the time to review the evidence that led to my freedom and admitted that she had been wrong about me all along.[2] Her apology touched me deeply, as i understood the pain her family had endured and the courage it took for her to embrace the truth. To Kolleen and the entire Schoen family, i extend my deepest gratitude. While you have suffered a tragic loss of a brother due to injustice, please know that

---

2 The Author and Kolleen's first in person meeting was featured the true crime podcast *Suspects: Five Shoots in the Dark,* "Episode 9," available on Spotify.

you have gained another one in me through love.

Lastly, one of the most courageous and honorable figures in my exoneration was Marion County Superior Court Judge, Shatrese Flowers. The circumstances of my case were unprecedented, as my legal team had exhausted all legal avenues for appeal, and it seemed unlikely that i would be granted another opportunity to be heard in court. The decision made by Judge Flowers carried immense weight. As an African American woman in a predominantly white and conservative Indiana Judicial system, she faced political pressure but remained steadfast in her commitment to justice. On March 8, 2023, she ordered my release and declared my innocence.

However, due to overwhelming sensations that my newly restored freedom had brought me after 25 years, it wasn't until 7 months later that i thought of reaching out to Flowers. i regret not having connected with her sooner, and it pained me to the core that she suddenly passed away on November 5, 2023, at the young age of 50, after battling a long-term illness.

My attending her funeral on November 14, 2023, was the first i had attended since my release. It was sublime almost. i had the opportunity to meet her husband, Kevin L. Moore, her mother, Melissa L. Flowers, and her sister, Sharonda Flowers-Rogers. Her husband embraced me like a brother and shared that she had wanted to meet me before her passing. During the service, i couldn't help but cry, torn between the guilt for not making the effort to meet her earlier and admiration for the profound impact she had made on countless lives. i couldn't help but notice the abundance of flowers at the funeral, which made me realize that regret often leads to more flowers being given to the deceased than gratitude does for the living. i shook my head in disappointment at my own thoughts.

In the end, i am still torn between gratitude and regret. My regret is that i will never be able to personally meet and thank Judge Flowers for what she has done for me and my family. However, i am eternally grateful, because i feel as though she is resting peacefully with the Ancestors, knowing that she gave me my flowers when she had the chance.

In conclusion, all these individuals and events have had a profound impact on my life, and i am filled with the deepest sense of gratitude towards each of them. From George Floyd, whose *blood sacrifice* brought attention to the flaws in our justice system and led to the establishment of conviction integrity units, to Mayor Joe Hogsett and Hampton Shields, who offered me a warm welcome back into the community. From Kollen Schoen-Bunch taking the time to meet with me despite the pain her family has had to endure and her courage in acknowledging my innocence has brought me healing and a sense of belonging, to Judge Flowers bring an example of steadfast and swift justice has seeded in my heart the intentions of creating the *gardens of* empathy, gratitude, love, and justice, whenever and wherever i have the chance to do so.

These letters of gratitude were but petals of encouragement from my soul, in my attempt to remind others that no matter what hardship you are experiencing, there is always hope if you can be grateful for the smallest acts of kindness.

Truth Never Dies,

LB

About the Author

Leon Benson still lives with the hope that his story will help in the setting of a national tone for the restorative justice initiatives desperately needed to repair the criminal justice system—the beginning of an atonement for what was taken from him.

Since his release, he has been attending events as both an emcee and a guest speaker, and has been engaging with other directly impacted communities to cultivate awareness. What sets Leon apart is his unwavering commitment to service-driven leadership. He understands that creativity and community-building are not mutually exclusive pursuits, but, rather, interdependent forces that can fuel positive change.

By harnessing the power of his creativity, Leon leverages his platform to shed light on important social issues, fostering dialogue and inspiring collective thinking and action.

WWW.LEONBENSON.ORG.

www.ingramcontent.com/pod-product-compliance
Lightning Source LLC
LaVergne TN
LVHW041631070526
838199LV00052B/3311